Did Y...

SWANSEA

A MISCELLANY

Compiled by Julia Skinner

With particular reference to the work of Tony Cornish

THE FRANCIS FRITH COLLECTION

www.francisfrith.com

First published in the United Kingdom in 2006 by The Francis Frith Collection®

This edition published exclusively for Oakridge Books & Gifts in 2010 ISBN 978-1-84589-550-1
Oakridge, Greenstalls Park, Costello Hill, Ilchester, Somerset BA22 8LB. Tel: 08453 893293

Text and Design copyright The Francis Frith Collection®
Photographs copyright The Francis Frith Collection® except where indicated.

The Frith® photographs and the Frith® logo are reproduced under licence from
Heritage Photographic Resources Ltd, the owners of the Frith® archive and trademarks.
'The Francis Frith Collection', 'Francis Frith' and 'Frith' are registered trademarks of
Heritage Photographic Resources Ltd.

British Library Cataloguing in Publication Data

Did You Know? Swansea - A Miscellany
Compiled by Julia Skinner
With particular reference to the work of Tony Cornish

The Francis Frith Collection
Frith's Barn, Teffont,
Salisbury, Wiltshire SP3 5QP
Tel: +44 (0) 1722 716 376
Email: info@francisfrith.co.uk
www.francisfrith.com

Printed and bound in England

Front Cover: **SWANSEA, WIND STREET AND VIVIAN STATUE 1896** 38754p

The colour-tinting is for illustrative purposes only, and is not intended to be historically accurate

CONTENTS

INTRODUCTION

To the casual visitor Swansea appears to be a very modern place, but it has a history stretching back many centuries. The area was used by the Vikings, and in later years the Normans built a castle here and developed the harbour.

During the Middle Ages the population of Swansea probably did not exceed about 1,500 people, but it was considered to be a major town in Wales. Its economy was mainly based on agriculture and fishing, but there was also a significant shipbuilding industry. In later centuries the town developed as demand for coal grew (there were many coalfields in the area), and with the introduction of copper smelting. By the 1800s, copper, zinc, steel and iron were all smelted in the town and over 6,000 ships were visiting Swansea every year. The port, and the various extensions of it to accommodate ever bigger ships and greater volumes of cargo, drove the vigorous economic development of the town.

Swansea's feeling of modernity is mostly attributable to the extensive rebuilding programmes that took place during the 1950s and 1960s, after the devastation of the Second World War. Swansea suffered a total of 44 air raids during the war, the most destructive of which was the three-night blitz of February 1941, which caused extensive damage: 112,000 buildings were destroyed or damaged, and 230 people were killed. As a significant port, Swansea was an obvious target - its docks, industry, flour mills and large grain stores were considered vital to the war effort.

One of Swansea's most famous sons, the poet Dylan Thomas, was born at 5 Cwmdonkin Drive in 1914 and raised in Uplands. He worked for the Swansea Evening Post, and Swansea was for him 'an ugly, lovely town, crawling, sprawling, slummed, unplanned, jerry-villaed and smug-suburbed by the side of a long and splendidly curving

shore'. Thomas obviously had mixed feelings about his birthplace, but today's visitor will find that Swansea is a bustling, modern city, a result of considerable investment as part of a plan to regenerate and redefine the city for the 21st century. The dockland areas have been extensively redeveloped as a leisure centre and marina, and the exciting National Waterfront Museum opened in October 2005. Swansea is now a commercial centre, and new industries have created increased employment opportunities.

The story of Swansea is full of fascinating characters and events, of which this book can only provide a brief glimpse.

HIGH STREET 1893 32720

WELSH WORDS
AND LOCAL PHRASES

The 2001 census found that 13.4% of Swansea's inhabitants were Welsh speakers, compared with 11% for the capital city of Wales, Cardiff. Here are a few Welsh phrases:

'Thank you' is *'Diolch'*.

'Good Health' or *'Cheers'* is *'Iechyd Da'*.

'Hello' is *'Shw mae'*.

'Goodbye' is *'Hwyl'*.

'Good morning' is *'Bore da'*.

'Good day' is *'Dydd da'*.

'How are you?' is *'Shwd i chi?'*.

'Very well, thank you' is *'Da iawn, diolch yn fawr'*.

'What is your name?' is *'Beth yw'ch enw chi?'*.

'Do you live here?' is *'Ydych chi'n byw yma?'*.

A local nickname for people from Swansea is *'Swansea Jacks'*. This may be a reminder of Swansea's former importance as a port, from the use of the word 'jack' for a sailor, but some people believe it is a reference to Swansea Jack, a famous life-saving dog (see page 29). The supporters of the Swans, Swansea City AFC, are known as **the Jack Army**.

SPOOKY SWANSEA

Swansea's Grand Theatre is haunted by a mysterious white, floating female figure. There are several theories about who she is: some say that she is the shade of Dame Adelina Patti, the famous 19th-century opera singer who lived at Craig-y-Nors; others say that she is the ghost of a young actress who appeared in a play for the last time at Swansea before travelling to America on the 'Titanic', and drowning when the great liner hit an iceberg and sank; and yet another story says that she is the ghost of a former wardrobe assistant at the theatre.

Swansea is famous for a carved wooden statue of a devil known as 'Old Nick', which is linked with some strange stories. Many people who see it find the statue disturbing, which seems to have been the intention of the architect who commissioned it. The story goes that the architect lost a contract to redesign St Mary's Church in the late 19th century, and built a building opposite the church, with this statue on top, saying 'My devil will be able to leer and laugh, for at some time in the future he will see St Mary's burned to the ground'. During the Second World War this prophecy came true, for Old Nick and the building that he guarded survived the blitz of 1941, although many surrounding buildings, including St Mary's, were destroyed. Old Nick was later installed over the entrance to the Quadrant Shopping Centre, but was removed from this position when the centre was redeveloped. There have been calls for him to be reinstated in a more prominent site, but if you look carefully you can still see him, peeping out from a perch high above the Whitewalls entrance to the shopping centre - still looking towards St Mary's.

Oystermouth Road is haunted by a strange white figure which is seen in the depths of the night; and Oystermouth Castle itself is haunted by a ghostly white lady, who walks along the top of the castle walls.

SWANSEA MISCELLANY

Tradition has it that Sweyn Forkbeard, King of Denmark in 1013, settled on an island here and gave the name of 'Sweyn's ey' to the immediate area ('ey' or 'ea' means 'inlet' or 'island'). Old drawings do indeed confirm that the River Tawe once divided to pass either side of a small islet in the mouth of the river. This would have made an excellent defensive site.

Before Swansea became an industrial centre, it became famous in the 18th century as a seaside resort and a place of elegance and culture; the town was described as 'the Brighton of Wales' (Gloucester Journal, 1786) and 'Bath by the sea'. Swansea is also the gateway to the beautiful Gower Peninsula, which was the first designated Area of Outstanding Beauty in Britain.

In the 1720s the writer and traveller Daniel Defoe visited Swansea and commented that it was 'a very considerable town and has a good harbour. There is also very great trade for coal which they export to all the ports of Somerset, Devon and Cornwall and also to Ireland itself so that one sometimes sees a hundred sail of ships at a time loading coal here which greatly enriches the country and particularly the town of Swansea'.

THE SANDS 1910 62573

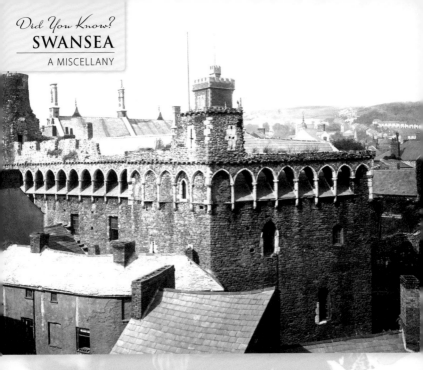

THE CASTLE 1893 32724

The Normans recognised the strategic importance of the Swansea area. In 1106 Henry de Beaumont arrived; he was the Earl of Warwick and newly appointed Lord of Gwyr, or Gower, and by 1116 he had built a castle on a small knoll near the river, a timber and turf structure defended by a system of ditches and banks. In 1116 an army of Welsh soldiers rampaged through Gower and attacked the castle; they were fended off, but in 1192 the castle was besieged for ten weeks, and the castle was again attacked in 1215 and 1217 - in the later attack the castle was destroyed.

In about 1330 Bishop Henry de Gower built another castle - more accurately a fortified house - at Swansea. This was severely damaged in the early 15th century during an attack by the Welsh freedom fighter Owain Glyndwr, and most of it was later demolished by the Parliamentarians in 1647, during the Civil War. All that is left to be seen today is a large tower and some domestic buildings. Much of High Street, Wind Street and St Mary's Church would once have been within the outer castle wall.

The now-demolished building on the right of photograph S240235, below, was the offices of the Swansea Evening Post at the time the photograph was taken. The building had variously been the Town Hall, a factory, a jail and a post office.

THE CASTLE GARDENS c1965 S240235

SOUTH DOCK 1906 54952

The South Dock opened in 1859, serving vessels for regular service to London, Bristol, Liverpool, Dublin and Cork. The ship shown in this photograph is the 'Talbot'. The shed seen in the photograph survived the wartime blitz and now houses the Maritime Museum; its gable end reads: 'Coast Lines Ltd. Sailings to and from all the principal ports of the United Kingdom. Shed 21'. The rail carriages in front linked the port facilities via a spur line to the GWR network.

KING'S DOCK 1925 77356

In the 19th century all kinds of shipments left Swansea for destinations all over the world, with cargoes from copper ore and coal to potatoes and onions. When sail gave way to steam, a bigger dock was needed, and King's Dock was built. Work began in July 1904; the dock was fully open in 1909, and was soon handling almost six million tonnes of goods per year.

The River Tawe used to run under Swansea's castle walls, but was re-routed when the port was enlarged by the digging of the New Cut; thus the North Dock was created, which opened to traffic in the summer of 1852.

Much of Swansea's architectural heritage was destroyed during the Second World War, and there are now only two remaining medieval buildings still surviving: the remains of the castle and the Cross Keys Inn.

In the 20th century the advent of oil-fired ships, trains, power stations and the increasing demand for petrol meant that the importation of oil for refineries had to be accommodated at the docks. Photograph 77366, below, shows the 'British Consul' out of London being shepherded into King's Dock by a Swansea tug.

AN OIL TANKER WITH A TUG ENTERING KING'S DOCK 1925 77366

The photograph of Wind Street opposite shows the Vivian Statue
in its original position; it has now been relocated and stands in St
Mary's Square. Sir Henry Hussey Vivian, born in 1821, was created the
first Baron Swansea in 1893, and died in 1894. The Vivian family were
central to the development of the fortunes of the town, being much
involved in the copper smelting industry.

In 1814 a pottery company in Swansea, Dillwyn & Co, began
making an especially beautiful type of porcelain. Swansea
Porcelain was made of soft paste, with a particularly
attractive colour, glaze and decoration. The most famous
decoration on the china consisted of flowers, painted by
William Billingsley. Swansea Porcelain is now rare and highly
prized by collectors, and examples can be seen in the Glyn
Vivian Art Gallery in the city.

In 1848, Charles Cunliffe wrote: 'The Swansea valley forms no bad
representation of the infernal regions, for the smell aids the eye.
Large groups of odd chimneys and rackety flues emit sulphurous,
arsenical smoke or pure flame. A dense canopy overhangs the scene
for several miles, rendered more horrible by the peculiar lurid glare.
All vegetation is blasted on the valley and adjoining hills. On a clear
day the smoke of Swansea valley may be seen at a distance of forty
or fifty miles and sometimes appears like a dense thundercloud'.

WIND STREET AND THE VIVIAN STATUE 1896 38754

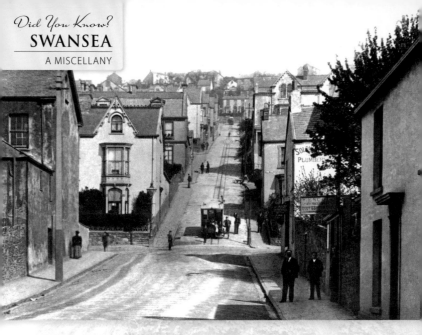

THE CLIFF TRAM, CONSTITUTIONAL HILL 1898 40920

The Constitutional Hill Railway, seen in photograph 40920, above, was constructed by the Incline Tramway Co, established in 1897. This feat of engineering was actually refused a Board of Trade certificate, and was later abandoned.

Swansea was attacked by enemy air raids 44 times during the Second World War, but the worst raids were on 19, 20 and 21 February 1941 when thousands of bombs and incendiaries were dropped on the town. The incendiaries caused the majority of the damage, and the fires acted as a homing beacon for successive waves of German bombers to locate the town and deliver more damage. The fires of Swansea could be seen from as far away as Pembrokeshire and North Devon. The death toll was 230, with 400 injured.

Swansea's old Guildhall at Somerset Place, seen in photograph 54950, below, was variously the site of executions, a school, a courthouse and a venue for Swansea's Literature Festival (a new Guildhall was opened in 1934). Most recently it has been used as the Dylan Thomas Centre, with exhibition, conference centre, restaurant and bar facilities. The centre was opened in 1995 by Jimmy Carter, ex-President of the USA, a great admirer of the work of Dylan Thomas.

THE GUILDHALL 1906 54950

The parish of Llansamlet is within Swansea's industrial catchment area, overlooking the Tawe valley. It was built principally on its tin-plate and spelter works. Although the area developed rapidly in the

19th century it has been a settlement for much longer. The parish of Llansamlet derives its name from the 7th-century St Samlet, and Llansamlet simply means 'Samlet's town' or 'Samlet's enclosure'.

LLANSAMLET, HEOL LAS 1938 88275

HIGH STREET 1910 62568

As 19th-century Swansea outgrew its water supply, the Board of Health remedied the situation by building two reservoirs, one at Brynmill and one at Cwmdonkin. To avoid the surplus land around the Cwmdonkin reservoir being built on (and thereby possibly contaminating the reservoir), it was decided to create a park and 'to set the land out as a public boon', according to a notice in The Cambrian.

The Brangwyn Hall at Swansea's Guildhall is noteworthy for its magnificent and colourful Empire Murals, which were created by the artist Frank Brangwyn. Brangwyn, who had Welsh connections on his father's side, had studied with William Morris and was an official First World War artist. His series of murals was originally commissioned by the House of Lords to decorate the Royal Gallery of the Palace of Westminster as a commemoration of the war, with 'decorative painting representing various Dominions and parts of the British Empire'. The finished result was thought to be too colourful and fantastical for the planned location and was declined by the client, and although the murals were completed and exhibited at the Daily Mail Ideal Home Exhibition in 1933, a new location was sought for the work. The murals were snapped up by Swansea to decorate the new Guildhall that was being built (which opened in 1934), and the ceiling of the Assembly Hall was specially raised to accommodate them.

In Oystermouth churchyard is the grave of Thomas Bowdler (1754-1825), whose expurgated version of the works of William Shakespeare gave the term 'to bowdlerise' to the English language.

Census records show that in 1801 Swansea's total population was 19,794; in 1901 it had risen to 153,577, and by 2001 the population was 223,293. By contrast, better healthcare, nutrition and lifestyles have resulted in the rate of infant mortality declining over the same period: the census for 1851 found that 132 babies in every thousand in Swansea died in their first year; by 1911 the number had only gone down to 130 in every thousand, but by the 2001 census the rate was seven in every thousand.

Swansea has a long tradition of stained-glass design and manufacture, and a particularly poignant example can be seen in the Lifeboat Window of All Saints' Church, Oystermouth. The window was designed by Tim Lewis, who was head of the School of Architectural Glass at Swansea, and commemorates the crew of the Mumbles Lifeboat who perished on 23 April 1947. During a severe storm the 7,000-ton SS 'Samtampa' was driven onto the rocks at Sker Point off Porthcawl, where she quickly broke up into three large pieces. Rescue rockets were fired to try and rescue the crew by breeches buoy, but the wind was too strong and the lines fell short of the ship. The Mumbles lifeboat was launched and reached the stricken ship, but capsized in the heavy sea. The lifeboat was later found upside down on the rocks not very far from the wrecked 'Samtampa', whose crew they had tried so bravely to rescue. All 30 crew of the 'Samtampa' were lost, and so were the eight-strong crew of the Mumbles lifeboat. All the bodies were found washed ashore the next day.

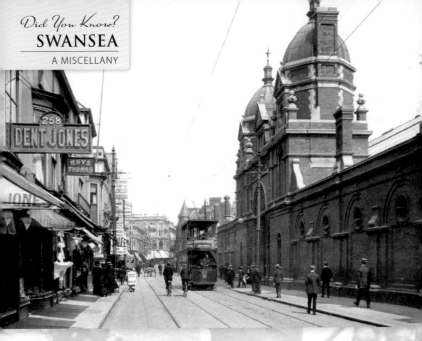

OXFORD STREET 1910 62566

The Victorian market building seen in photograph 62566, above, was claimed to be the largest covered market in Britain in its day. It was badly damaged in the three-night blitz of Swansea in 1941. Swansea's present-day Central Market is believed to be the largest covered market in Wales.

Swansea Bay was the scene of two occasions of public hangings (of three people in total) in the 19th century. The second occasion attracted over 15,000 spectators. A fairground added to the spectacle, and over 100 onlookers were injured when they fought to gain a closer viewpoint.

The first copper works were established in the area in 1717; Swansea was once humorously referred to as 'Copperopolis'.

The Civic Buildings in Victoria Park, seen in photograph S240209, below, were designed by Sir Percy Thomas, started in 1930 and opened in 1934. The design was controversial at the time, and is representative of the modern movement in architecture; it has been described as having a 'stripped classical' style. Notice the prow of a Viking longboat in the clock-tower, a reminder of Sweyn Forkbeard's links with the city (see page 6).

THE CIVIC BUILDINGS c1960 S240209

The Mumbles, a few miles from Swansea, became popular in
the 19th century as a resort for people seeking to escape the
industrial grime of the city. Part of its success was owed to the first
and one of the longest-running passenger railway services in the

OFF TO THE MUMBLES 1899 43670a

world; this was opened between The Mumbles and Swansea in 1807, and originally used horses as the motive power. The railway was closed in 1960.

ST MARY'S CHURCH 1899 43668

ST MARY'S CHURCH c1965 S240249B

The Victorian St Mary's Church shown in photograph 43668 (opposite top) was gutted in the 1941 blitz, when its timber roof was destroyed by incendiary bombs. The building was faithfully restored between 1954-59 under the auspices of Sir Percy Thomas. The new church, seen in photograph S240249B (opposite below), was opened by Queen Elizabeth the Queen Mother on 28 May 1959.

A monument on the Promenade near the St Helen's ground commemorates a black retriever called Jack, who became nationally famous as a life-saving dog. Born in 1930, during his lifetime he is said to have saved 27 people from drowning in Swansea docks, and was given the title 'Bravest Dog of the Year' by the Star newspaper in 1936. Jack died in 1937 after eating rat poison, and the monument commemorating him was erected by public subscription. He was awarded two bronze medals, the canine version of the VC, by the National Canine Defence League, the only dog so far to have received this honour. The Swansea Jack pub in Oystermouth Road is named after him.

Before the more prudish Victorian era, nude bathing was not unusual. J T Barber commented in 1803 on the liberated women of the Swansea area: 'As we were strolling on the sands we remarked a group of female figures in birthday attire gambolling in the water. In our subsequent rambles on the beach these liberal exhibitions of Cambrian beauty afforded us many pleasing studies of unsophisticated nature'.

VICTORIA PARK, THE PATTI PAVILION 1925 77383

The Pavilion in Victoria Park, seen in photograph 77383, above, is there as a result of a donation by the operatic diva Madame Adelina Patti, one of the most famous and successful opera singers in the world in the late 19th century. Madame Patti had a mansion nearby, Craig-y-Nos; she made extensive alterations and extensions to the house, and added a winter garden. In 1918, just before her death in 1919, Madame Patti gave the winter garden building to the people of Swansea, and in 1920 it was re-erected in Victoria Park, becoming known as the Patti Pavilion. It was once home to the Welsh National Opera. The elaborate portico seen in the photograph has now been blocked in.

Photograph 32731, below, shows the famous lighthouse on Middle Head, The Mumbles. Built in 1794, the lighthouse originally had two platforms, each with a coal-fired beacon to warn shipping of the dangers of the Mixon Sands and Cherry Stone Rock. In 1799 it became oil-fired, and it was converted to electricity in 1905. The last keeper retired in 1934 when it became an automatic light.

THE MUMBLES, THE LIGHTHOUSE 1893 32731

Did You Know?

SWANSEA

A MISCELLANY

Photograph 40925 shows the terminus of the Swansea to Mumbles railway at Mumbles pier, which was essential for the recreation of Victorian and Edwardian visitors to this part of the seaside. The pier was also the embarkation point for paddle steamers.

THE MUMBLES, THE PIER 1898 40925

PONTARDDULAIS, THE VIADUCT c1955 P165004

THE MUMBLES, OYSTERMOUTH CASTLE 1893 32739

The viaduct at Pontarddulais, seen in photograph P165004, opposite, was a vital link in the industrial network of the Swansea area, helping to transport coal and thereby service the local iron, copper, zinc and tin industries.

Situated four miles south-west of Swansea overlooking Swansea Bay, Oystermouth Castle is one of the most intact castles in Gower. The name derives from a Norman/English corruption of Ystumllwynarth. The first stronghold on the site was probably built by Henry de Beaumont, Earl of Warwick, following his being made Lord of Gower by Henry I. Following its destruction after an uprising in 1287, Oystermouth was rebuilt as a courtyard castle. At one end was a three-storey gatehouse whose top floor was occupied by a large chapel. At the other end was the rectangular tower, the remains of which are the subject of photograph 32739, opposite. The two structures were linked together by a high curtain wall. Remodelling went on into the 16th century. 'There is in this parish a very spacious castle having many dry Roomes, vaults and sellers in it, with staires, towers and walkes very firm, in some arches there are flowes and coates of arms painted in divers colours'. (Isaac Hamon, in the 1690s.)

The Glass Leaf sculpture in Swansea's Castle Square is by the local artist Amber Hiscott, and was unveiled on 27 November 1996. Around the pool edge is an inscription from Dylan Thomas's poem 'Rain Cuts the Place We Tread', in which the poet recalled playing with leaves in Cwmdonkin Park as a child, making them into boats to sail in puddles: 'We sail a boat upon the path, paddle with leaves, down an ecstatic line of light.'

THE GENERAL AND EYE HOSPITAL 1893 32722

Did You Know?
SWANSEA
A MISCELLANY

SPORTING SWANSEA

In 1998, to mark 100 seasons of league football, the Football League published a list of 100 football legends. The list contained four Swansea-born men, who all began their careers at their home-town club. The four were Ivor Allchurch, John Charles, Trevor Ford, and Cliff Jones.

The St Helen's ground in Swansea is, if not unique, very unusual in having staged international fixtures in three sports. One-day international cricket was played at the ground in the 1970s, and the Welsh team played full rugby union internationals here for many years. International rugby league has also been played here. One of the most famous matches to take place at St Helen's was the rugby union match between Swansea and the All Blacks in 1935. Swansea won 11-3, to become the first British club side to beat the New Zealanders. One of the most memorable incidents in cricket at the ground was the occasion in 1968 when Gary Sobers became the first player ever to score six 'sixes' in an over in first-class cricket, playing for Nottinghamshire against Glamorgan.

Swansea Rugby Club has a long list of achievements, but the success of the 1904/05 'Invincibles' side is as great as any. Playing against the best clubs in Wales and England, they won 27 and drew 4 of their 31 games. This great consistency was based on extraordinary defence. They conceded just 51 points all season, including 21 games where no points were conceded at all. Over the season, six of the club's players were selected for the national team.

One of the finest boxers that Wales has produced was Swansea-born Colin Jones. He was a hard-hitting welterweight, who lost only three fights. Sadly, a world title just eluded him. The nearest that he came to it was a drawn fight against Milton McCrory, in Nevada. Jones lost the re-match five months later in August 1983, after a controversial split decision.

QUIZ QUESTIONS

Answers on page 48.

1. What is the Welsh name for Swansea, and what does it mean?

2. Where in Swansea can you find the faces of Sir Winston Churchill and Field Marshall Montgomery carved in wood?

3. What important event for Swansea occurred in 1969?

4. What is the link between Swansea and Dr Who?

5. Swansea is twinned with which three places?

6. What is 'Olga', and where can you find her?

7. Who were known as Swansea Cape Horners?

8. What was the Red Lady of Paviland?

9. Which is the oldest pub in Swansea?

10. Which king was King's Dock named after?

Did You Know?
SWANSEA
A MISCELLANY

RECIPE

GLAMORGAN SAUSAGES

Ingredients

150g/5oz fresh breadcrumbs
150g/5oz grated Caerphilly cheese
1 small leek, very finely chopped
1 tablespoonful chopped fresh parsley
Leaves from 1 sprig of thyme, chopped

2 eggs
1½ teaspoonfuls mustard powder
3 tablespoonfuls milk
Plain flour, for coating
1 tablespoonful oil
1 tablespoonful melted butter
Salt and pepper

Mix the breadcrumbs, cheese, leek, herbs and seasoning. Whisk the eggs with the mustard and reserve 2 tablespoonfuls of the mixture. Stir the rest into the cheese mixture with enough milk to bind. Divide the cheese mixture into eight and form into sausage shapes. Dip the sausages in the reserved egg to coat. Season the flour, then roll the sausages in it to give a light, even coating. Chill for about 30 minutes until firm. Preheat the grill and oil the grill rack. Mix the oil and melted butter together and brush over the sausages. Grill the sausages for about 5-10 minutes, turning carefully, until golden brown all over. Serve hot or cold.

CASTLE STREET 1925 77379

LESLIE
BAKERY &
Refreshment
Rooms

MAKER
OF

TOBACCO

BATHS

STEAM LAUNDRY

RECIPE

TEISEN SINAMON - WELSH CINNAMON CAKE

Ingredients

225g/8oz plain flour
½ teaspoonful baking powder
110g/4oz caster sugar
110g/4oz butter
3 eggs, separated into yolks and whites

1 teaspoonful ground cinnamon
3 further tablespoonfuls caster sugar
Jam of your choice, ie raspberry, strawberry, apricot
Enough milk to mix - approx 6 tablespoonfuls

Pre-heat the oven to 200 degrees C/400 degrees F/Gas Mark 6.

Sieve the flour, cinnamon and baking powder into a large mixing bowl. Rub in the butter and 110g/4oz sugar. Add the beaten egg yolks and enough milk to make a stiff mixture - it should still be quite firm. Spoon the mixture into a well greased baking tin or ovenproof dish which the cake can also be served in. Bake for 20-25 minutes until cooked, then allow to cool for at least 30 minutes in the tin.

Make a meringue topping by whisking the egg whites until stiff, and then fold in the three tablespoonfuls of caster sugar. Spread the top of the cooled cake with jam of your choice, and then spread the meringue on top of this.

Reduce the heat of the oven to 170 degrees C/ 325 degrees F/Gas Mark 3. Bake the cake for around 20 minutes or until the meringue is firm and light golden on the peaks. Serve either hot or cold, but it is best eaten straight away, before the jam makes the cake soggy.

QUIZ ANSWERS

1. The Welsh name for Swansea is Abertawe, which means 'At the mouth of the Tawe'.

2. In St Mary's Church. When the church was re-consecrated having being restored after the Second World War, the two humorous woodcarvings shown in photograph S240247A on page 50 were put in place. They depict two war heroes: Churchill, complete with characteristic hat and cigar on the left, and Montgomery on the right.

3. Swansea was granted city status in 1969, as part of the celebrations marking the investiture of Prince Charles as Prince of Wales.

4. Russell T Davies, who is executive producer and chief writer of the award-winning revival of the 'Dr Who' series, was born in Swansea in 1963.

5. Swansea is twinned with Mannheim in Germany, Pau in France and Cork in the Republic of Ireland.

6. 'Olga' is one of the vessels in the collection of Swansea Museum, and can be seen during June, July and August at the Swansea Marina. The entrance to the pontoon can be found near the Waterfront Tavern on Museum Square. 'Olga' is a rare survivor from Swansea's maritime past, and is listed on the National Historic Ships Committee Core Collection list. She was built in 1909, and was used as a Pilot Cutter, taking pilots out to guide larger ships through the treacherous waters of the Bristol Channel.

7. 'Cape Horners' was the name given to Swansea seamen who had successfully made the journey around Cape Horn to Chile, taking out cargoes of Welsh coal and returning with Chilean copper for Swansea's copper smelting industry. The difficult and highly dangerous journey usually took about one year in the days of sail.

8. The Red Lady of Paviland is the name given to a headless human skeleton which was found in 1823 in Goat's Hole, Paviland, on the Gower Peninsular. The discovery was made by Dean Buckland, the Professor of Geology at the University of Oxford. He believed the skeleton to be of a female, and named it 'the Red Lady' as it was dyed with the red ochre that had been used on the body as part of the funeral rites. The skeleton has since been identified as a male. Radiocarbon dating has shown that the remains date from around 26,000BC, making them the oldest human remains found in the United Kingdom; the find is also the oldest known ceremonial burial so far found in Western Europe. The Red Lady is now displayed at Oxford University Natural History Museum, although there have been suggestions that the remains should be kept in Swansea Museum.

9. The Cross Keys Inn, the oldest medieval surviving tavern in Swansea, on an alley off Wind Street.

10. King's Dock was named after Edward VII; he and Queen Alexandra visited Swansea on 20 July 1904 to cut the first sod.

ST MARY'S CHURCH, THE TWO HEADS c1965 S240247A

THE SANDS 1925 77375

OYSTERMOUTH CASTLE 1893 32737

TWALTER ROAD 1906 54948

HALFORD
CYCLE CO

FRANCIS FRITH

PIONEER VICTORIAN PHOTOGRAPHER

Francis Frith, founder of the world-famous photographic archive, was a complex and multi-talented man. A devout Quaker and a highly successful Victorian businessman, he was philosophical by nature and pioneering in outlook. By 1855 he had already established a wholesale grocery business in Liverpool, and sold it for the astonishing sum of £200,000, which is the equivalent today of over £15,000,000. Now in his thirties, and captivated by the new science of photography, Frith set out on a series of pioneering journeys up the Nile and to the Near East.

INTRIGUE AND EXPLORATION

He was the first photographer to venture beyond the sixth cataract of the Nile. Africa was still the mysterious 'Dark Continent', and Stanley and Livingstone's historic meeting was a decade into the future. The conditions for picture taking confound belief. He laboured for hours in his wicker dark-room in the sweltering heat of the desert, while the volatile chemicals fizzed dangerously in their trays. Back in London he exhibited his photographs and was 'rapturously cheered' by members of the Royal Society. His reputation as a photographer was made overnight.

VENTURE OF A LIFE-TIME

By the 1870s the railways had threaded their way across the country, and Bank Holidays and half-day Saturdays had been made obligatory by Act of Parliament. All of a sudden the working man and his family were able to enjoy days out, take holidays, and see a little more of the world.

With typical business acumen, Francis Frith foresaw that these new tourists would enjoy having souvenirs to commemorate their days out. For the next thirty years he travelled the country by train and by pony and trap, producing fine photographs of seaside resorts and beauty spots that were keenly bought by millions of Victorians. These prints were painstakingly pasted into family albums and pored over during the dark nights of winter, rekindling precious memories of summer excursions. Frith's studio was soon supplying retail shops all over the country, and by 1890 F Frith & Co had become the greatest specialist photographic publishing company in the world, with over 2,000 sales outlets, and pioneered the picture postcard.

FRANCIS FRITH'S LEGACY

Francis Frith had died in 1898 at his villa in Cannes, his great project still growing. By 1970 the archive he created contained over a third of a million pictures showing 7,000 British towns and villages.

Frith's legacy to us today is of immense significance and value, for the magnificent archive of evocative photographs he created provides a unique record of change in the cities, towns and villages throughout Britain over a century and more. Frith and his fellow studio photographers revisited locations many times down the years to update their views, compiling for us an enthralling and colourful pageant of British life and character.

We are fortunate that Frith was dedicated to recording the minutiae of everyday life. For it is this sheer wealth of visual data, the painstaking chronicle of changes in dress, transport, street layouts, buildings, housing and landscape that captivates us so much today, offering us a powerful link with the past and with the lives of our ancestors.

Computers have now made it possible for Frith's many thousands of images to be accessed almost instantly. The archive offers every one of us an opportunity to examine the places where we and our families have lived and worked down the years. Its images, depicting our shared past, are now bringing pleasure and enlightenment to millions around the world a century and more after his death.

For further information visit: www.francisfrith.com

INTERIOR DECORATION

Frith's photographs can be seen framed and as giant wall murals in thousands of pubs, restaurants, hotels, banks, retail stores and other public buildings throughout Britain. These provide interesting and attractive décor, generating strong local interest and acting as a powerful reminder of gentler days in our increasingly busy and frenetic world.

FRITH PRODUCTS

All Frith photographs are available as prints and posters in a variety of different sizes and styles. In the UK we also offer a range of other gift and stationery products illustrated with Frith photographs, although many of these are not available for delivery outside the UK – see our web site for more information on the products available for delivery in your country.

THE INTERNET

Over 100,000 photographs of Britain can be viewed and purchased on the Frith web site. The web site also includes memories and reminiscences contributed by our customers, who have personal knowledge of localities and of the people and properties depicted in Frith photographs. If you wish to learn more about a specific town or village you may find these reminiscences fascinating to browse. Why not add your own comments if you think they would be of interest to others? See **www.francisfrith.com**

PLEASE HELP US BRING FRITH'S PHOTOGRAPHS TO LIFE

Our authors do their best to recount the history of the places they write about. They give insights into how particular towns and villages developed, they describe the architecture of streets and buildings, and they discuss the lives of famous people who lived there. But however knowledgeable our authors are, the story they tell is necessarily incomplete.

Frith's photographs are so much more than plain historical documents. They are living proofs of the flow of human life down the generations. They show real people at real moments in history; and each of those people is the son or daughter of someone, the brother or sister, aunt or uncle, grandfather or grandmother of someone else. All of them lived, worked and played in the streets depicted in Frith's photographs.

We would be grateful if you would give us your insights into the places shown in our photographs: the streets and buildings, the shops, businesses and industries. Post your memories of life in those streets on the Frith website: what it was like growing up there, who ran the local shop and what shopping was like years ago; if your workplace is shown tell us about your working day and what the building is used for now. Read other visitors' memories and reconnect with your shared local history and heritage. With your help more and more Frith photographs can be brought to life, and vital memories preserved for posterity, and for the benefit of historians in the future.

Wherever possible, we will try to include some of your comments in future editions of our books. Moreover, if you spot errors in dates, titles or other facts, please let us know, because our archive records are not always completely accurate—they rely on 140 years of human endeavour and hand-compiled records. You can email us using the contact form on the website.

Thank you!

For further information, trade, or author enquiries
please contact us at the address below:

The Francis Frith Collection, Frith's Barn, Teffont, Salisbury, Wiltshire, England SP3 5QP.

Tel: +44 (0)1722 716 376 Fax: +44 (0)1722 716 881
e-mail: sales@francisfrith.co.uk **www.francisfrith.com**